ON LINE

John Jay

by
Stuart A. Kallen

BIOGRAPHIES

Founding Fathers

Visit us at
www.abdopub.com

Published by ABDO Publishing Company, 4940 Viking Drive, Edina, MN 55435. Copyright ©2001 by Abdo Consulting Group, Inc. International copyrights reserved in all countries. No part of this book may be reproduced in any form without written permission from the publisher.

Printed in the United States.

Graphic design: John Hamilton
Cover Design: Maclean Tuminelly

Cover photo: Corbis
Interior photos and illustrations:
    Corbis: p. 11, 15, 21, 23, 25, 27, 29, 33, 35, 37, 40, 43, 47, 49, 54, 57, 59
    New York State Historical Association, p. 6
    North Wind Pictures: p. 5, 9, 13, 16, 19, 39, 45, 51

Library of Congress Cataloging-in-Publication Data

Kallen, Stuart A., 1955-
    John Jay / Stuart Kallen.
        p. cm. — (Founding fathers)
    Includes index.
    Summary: Discusses the life and political career of the man who was a delegate to the First Continental Congress, one of the authors of "The Federalist," and first Chief Justice of the Supreme Court.
    ISBN 1-57765-013-1
    1. Jay, John, 1745-1829—Juvenile literature.
2. Statesmen—United States—Biography—Juvenile literature. 3. United States—Politics and government—1775-1783—Juvenile literature. 4. United States—Politics and government—1783-1809—Juvenile literature.
5. Judges—New York (State)—Biography—Juvenile literature. 6. New York (State)—Politics and government—To 1775—Juvenile literature. [1. Jay, John, 1745-1829. 2. Statesmen.] I. Title.

E302.6.J4 K35 2001
973.3'092—dc21
[B]
                                                98-005724

Contents

Introduction

IT WAS JULY 1794. Angry Philadelphians gathered together in the streets of the city. From politicians to laborers, their voices and tempers rose in rage against one man. In the center of the crowd, a straw-filled dummy was brought forth. Someone hung a sign around its neck that said "John Jay." The crowd roared its approval as the effigy of Jay was hung from a tree. Screams, insults, and stones were hurled at the swaying replica of the man who was Chief Justice of the Supreme Court.

After several hours, the effigy was cut down. But the crowd's anger still raged. Taken to a guillotine, the dummy was placed on the instrument. The blade swooped down, and off rolled the straw-filled head. The mob roared with approval. Finally, the headless effigy was doused with rum and burned.

Facing page: a portrait of John Jay.

In 1794, in Philadelphia, Pennsylvania, an angry mob of colonists burned a straw dummy (an effigy) made to look like Supreme Court Chief Justice John Jay. The mob was angry over Jay's treaty with England.

> *John Jay once said that he could find his way across the country by the light of his effigies burning.*

This gruesome protest was aimed at the man who had just returned from London with a treaty that guaranteed America profits and peace with England.

Most Americans still hated England, since the bloody war for independence had ended only 11 years earlier. Thus, John Jay's peaceful and successful negotiations with Great Britain was not only *not* popular, it was hated.

Although shocked, John Jay forgave the mob. As a legal scholar and judge, he knew that this treaty was the right thing for America, the country he loved.

Rise of a New York Family

ONLY 5,000 PEOPLE lived in New York City at the turn of the eighteenth century. It was during this time that Augustus Jay moved to America to escape religious cruelty in his native France. Augustus belonged to a Protestant sect called the Huguenots. He married Anne Maria Bayard, the daughter of a rich merchant, and quickly became one of New York's wealthiest men.

Augustus had a son named Peter, who also became very rich. Peter Jay had large warehouses on New York's waterfront. They were piled high with a wide variety of items including deer hides, grain, pork, nails, oil, turpentine, wax, and tar.

Peter Jay bought his goods from America's farmers and merchants. He shipped the items to England, where they were sold. When his ships returned to New York they were loaded with English beer, ivory combs, silver buttons, fans, fishhooks, hats, spectacles, and clothing.

An eighteenth century map of New York City.

A Son is Born

JOHN JAY WAS BORN on December 12, 1745, to Peter and Mary van Courtlandt Jay. His birth was not an unusual event. John was the eighth child born to the Jay family. When he was eight years old, John was sent to New Rochelle school, where he studied the strict Huguenot religion along with calculus, Greek, Latin, and other subjects.

In 1760, when he was 14, John entered King's College (now Columbia University) in New York City. To get into this college, Jay was required to read six Latin books and give "a rational account of Latin and Greek grammar, and translate the first 10 chapters of St. John's Gospel from Greek to Latin."

While in college, Jay became interested in studying law. He graduated with highest honors from King's College, intent on becoming a lawyer.

The library at Columbia University. When John Jay attended school here, it was called King's College.

The Dreaded Stamp Act

I N 1764, THE YEAR JAY GRADUATED, America faced a serious situation. England and France had ended seven long years of fighting. (The French were aided by Native Americans, so the conflict became known in the colonies as "The French and Indian Wars.") These European countries were fighting over who controlled the untamed lands of Pennsylvania, Ohio, and other western territories. England finally won the long, bloody war, but the cost put the British deeply in debt. The English government, called Parliament, decided to raise money by taxing Americans.

England had been peacefully ruling the 13 American colonies for more than 150 years. But that was about to change. When Parliament passed the Stamp Act of 1765, Americans were outraged.

The colonies had no representatives in the British government when this tax was imposed. And suddenly they were told to pay taxes on everything printed from newspapers to playing cards. Colonials demanded that there should be "No taxation without representation!"

An example of a stamp the colonists were forced to buy and affix to printed literature, such as newspapers and playing cards.

Jay, the Law Clerk

ALTHOUGH THE STAMP ACT created a serious situation in the colonies, Jay's thoughts were centered on his first job. The young man began work as a law clerk in the offices of lawyer Benjamin Kissam. The job was difficult. There were no printed law forms in those days. Jay had to copy long, complicated legal documents by hand. However, Jay was an excellent clerk and rose quickly through the firm. Within two years, he was conducting routine legal business. Because Jay was so skilled at writing, he later left behind many documents for historians to study.

While John Jay did not concern himself with politics, his father Peter Jay did. Of the Stamp Act the elder man wrote, "Our colonists cannot digest the hard measure they are dealt with in Parliament."

As a young man, John Jay was an excellent law clerk.

THE FOLLY OF ENGLAND
AND THE RUIN OF AMERICA

In Boston, people strongly protested the Stamp Act. There were a few near-riots inspired by Samuel Adams. The Stamp Act was repealed by Parliament one year after it was enacted.

Americans celebrated the death of the Stamp Act. But their troubles were just beginning. In 1767, Parliament passed the Townsend Acts. This law placed a tax on glass, paint, paper, and America's favorite drink—tea. Once again, people in Boston fought back. They decided to boycott (stop buying) the taxed goods. Within a year, Parliament repealed the tax on everything except tea.

Meanwhile, in New York, John Jay received his license to practice law in October 1768. He must have been happy on his 23rd birthday. He was a successful lawyer from a wealthy family with connections in the highest reaches of New York society. He went to dances and parties, where he enjoyed the finest wines and foods. In his spare time, he played backgammon and cards. Jay was also very busy. By 1773, he was working on over 160 legal cases a year!

Facing page: Stamp Act riots in the streets of Boston, Massachusetts.

More Tea Troubles in the North

ALTHOUGH JAY'S CITY of New York had been pretty quiet during the tax troubles, this was not the case in Massachusetts. In 1773, three ships loaded with tea sailed into Boston Harbor. Angry Americans would not let workers unload the ships. Merchants refused to pay taxes on the tea. The governor of Massachusetts ordered the ships unloaded by December 16.

On that cold, rainy night a group of men boarded the tea ships. They wore feathers in their hair and painted their faces like Mohawk Indians. The men threw 342 chests of tea into Boston Harbor.

The Boston Tea Party outraged the British government. The British navy closed Boston Harbor. With no boats coming or going, Boston ran short of food. Businesses closed and the Massachusetts economy was in a shambles. New Yorkers wondered what would happen if the British did the same thing to them.

The Boston Tea Party.

Committee of 51

ALTHOUGH THE COUNTRY faced many serious issues, life continued. John Jay was busy thinking of his coming marriage. Jay married Sarah Van Brugh Livingston on April 28, 1774. Sarah was the daughter of William Livingston, a well-known lawyer in business and social circles in New York, and a member of the First and Second Continental Congresses.

In Boston, a group called the Sons of Liberty had organized to protest the British crackdown. New York also had a Sons of Liberty group. Because there were 51 members, the group was known as the Committee of 51. This committee was much less radical than its Boston cousin. Most members of the committee wanted to negotiate a peaceful settlement to the problem. However, Boston's patriots were ready for revolution.

John Jay was elected to the New York Sons of
Liberty and quickly became the leader. Jay called
for a general congress to discuss the "shocking and
detestable acts of Parliament that shuts up the Port
[of Boston]."

*Members of the Sons of Liberty get into a brawl
with British soldiers in Boston.*

The First Continental Congress

AS A MEMBER of the Committee of 51, Jay was elected to attend the First Continental Congress. The congress was held in Philadelphia in September 1774. Representatives from every colony except Georgia were there. At the age of 29, Jay was one of the youngest delegates. Unlike most of the other delegates, he had never been elected to public office.

Jay was among men of talent and fame. George Washington, Benjamin Franklin, Patrick Henry, and John Adams were just a few of the delegates. Some men at the congress wanted an all-out war with England. Others, like Jay, were moderates who wished to avoid armed conflict.

Delegates had much to disagree about and very little got done. Small states were afraid of the

Carpenters' Hall, in Philadelphia, Pennsylvania, site of the First Continental Congress.

power of large states. Some men wanted independence and others did not. One of the highlights of the congress was a letter written by Jay to the people of England. In it, he urged the British to reign in their Parliament. He said that their tactics threatened not only the colonists, but also the British themselves. At the end of the letter, Jay said that colonists would stop exporting goods to England if Parliament did not back down.

When the Continental Congress broke up at the end of October, they sent a list of demands to England. They wanted civil rights in the colonies. And they created a group of representatives from each colony to tighten the boycott on English goods.

War!

I N 1775, THE BRITISH decided to tighten their control on the colonies. On April 19, outside of Boston, British soldiers, nicknamed "redcoats," went to seize gunpowder belonging to American militiamen. Bloody battles erupted at Lexington and Concord. The Revolutionary War had begun.

On May 10, the Second Continental Congress met in Philadelphia. John Jay was there. George Washington, dressed in his military uniform, quietly announced he was ready to fight. On June 15, 1775, the 43-year-old Washington was unanimously elected general and commander-in-chief of the Continental Army.

Jay and other moderates, however, were still not ready for a total break with England. Jay suggested writing a petition to England's King George III asking for peace. This document, called the Olive Branch Petition, was sent to England. The Continental Congress closed in August. Jay returned home, hoping that his Olive Branch Petition would help make peace between England and America.

In England, however, King George was preparing 20,000 troops for battle. The king wrote that his plan for America was to "force those deluded people to submission [surrender]." King George refused to even look at Jay's Olive Branch Petition.

American minutemen fight British redcoats at the Battle of Concord.

Declaring Independence

A BRITISH WARSHIP attacked New York City on August 29, 1775. On September 5, Jay went to Philadelphia when the Second Continental Congress met once again. By the middle of November, New York City trade had come to a standstill. Half of the population had left in fear of British bombardment. Back in Philadelphia, Jay was serving on six congressional committees. He returned to New York City in January 1776.

The Jays had a son, Peter Augustus, on January 24. The birth caused health problems for Sarah. During this time, Jay was also elected to the New York Provincial Congress, but he spent most of his time by his wife's sickbed.

Meanwhile, the entire country was moving towards independence from England. Jay still

Artist John Trumbull's Signers of the Declaration of Independence.

opposed the idea. When delegates at the congress drew up a letter demanding separation from England, Jay wrote that independence would "create division and have an unhappy influence."

On July 4, 1776, delegates of the Continental Congress finalized the Declaration of Independence. The document, written by Thomas Jefferson, declared that America was free of English rule. Jay had remained in New York while the Declaration of Independence was introduced, debated, and adopted.

"The Risk of Our Lives and Fortunes"

BY JULY 9, 1776, Jay could not ignore signs of war. The mightiest military force ever deployed by a European nation (outside of Europe) was assembled off the coast of New York. A British fleet of 134 war vessels lay in the waters surrounding New York City. British soldiers, nearly 6,000 seasoned redcoats, were joined by 8,000 Hessian (German) soldiers on nearby Staten Island. From the north, 13,000 more redcoats marched in.

Jay finally understood that war was inevitable. He voted in the New York Congress to support the Declaration of Independence. He wrote: "We approve [of the Declaration] at the risk of our lives and fortunes, and join with the other colonies in supporting it."

By July 1776, British warships had surrounded New York City.

Jay soon became a full-fledged patriot. He headed a committee to punish people engaged in activities against the Continental Army. Men were rounded up for treason, counterfeiting, and aiding the enemy.

Jay also organized a spy ring. He placed spies among the ranks of British officers. He wrote letters in invisible ink, and he collected information about British troop movements.

New York Chief Justice

J AY'S NEXT CHALLENGE was to draft a constitution for the state of New York. Jay's constitution limited the power of the governor, and it had broad measures to insure religious freedom. New York continued to press Jay for his services. He was appointed as chief justice to the state Supreme Court. There, he oversaw trials of dozens of war crimes including murder, assault, counterfeiting, and grand larceny. Jay sentenced 10 men to hang—not an easy chore for a thoughtful man.

In December of 1778, Jay returned to the Continental Congress, where he was elected president. During his nine months as head of Congress, Jay dealt with many problems. The states argued with one another over money, territory, and trade. Money was short and prices were soaring. Jay reminded the states that they were honor bound to pay off the national debt. He called on them to raise taxes to pay for the war.

New York Supreme Court Chief Justice John Jay.

Treaty Troubles

F RANCE HAD BEEN AT WAR with England off and on for years, so it was no surprise that the French were glad to help the American cause. In 1778, France declared war on England and began funneling money, supplies, and soldiers into America.

While Jay was president of the Continental Congress, problems arose with treaties America had signed with France. France had agreed to fight Britain alongside the Americans, but France had secretly signed a treaty with Spain. That treaty said that France would give fishing rights in Newfoundland to Spain. In return, Spain said it would help France fight England.

Americans were shocked when they found out about France's treaty with Spain. Newfoundland was an area that Americans had fished for over 100 years. Even more seriously, the treaty called for America, France, and Spain to fight England until all parties agreed to end the war.

The treaty problems convinced Congress to send delegates to Europe to spell out America's peace aims. Congress wanted to send men who would put the public good ahead of private gain. The men chosen were Benjamin Franklin, John Adams, and John Jay. Franklin went to France; Adams went to England; and Jay went to Spain.

Jay and his wife set sail for Spain. But their ship was pounded by heavy gales. The ship's sails blew off and the masts fell over. The Jays were forced to land on the Caribbean isle of Martinique.

This map, printed in London just a month after the Declaration of Independence, shows Newfoundland in relation to the rest of the northern American colonies. (Map enhanced to show Newfoundland.)

The Jays in Spain

JAY LOVED THE BEAUTY of tropical Martinique. But he was sickened by the sight of slaves weighted down with iron collars around their necks. The slaves dragged 50-pound (22.7-kg) chains and had scars from whippings. Jay would never forget that sight when he became a strong anti-slavery leader years later.

The Jays finally reached Spain in January 1780. The king treated them rudely. Although the Jays stayed in Spain for two years, they were often ignored. Spain's king was afraid of America's version of independence. He didn't want Spanish colonies in Central and South America to have their own revolution. Spain's minister summed up the mission when he said, "Jay's two chief points were: Recognize our independence; give us more money." Jay wrote the trip was "one continued series of painful perplexities and embarrassments."

Meanwhile, Washington defeated the British at Yorktown, Virginia, on October 17, 1781. The American Revolution was over, and the colonies were free to rule themselves.

The Battle of Yorktown in October 1781, marked the end of the war for American independence.

The Paris Peace Treaty

BENJAMIN FRANKLIN sent for Jay in Spain. Jay was to go to France to help negotiate peace with England. The Jays were thrilled to leave Spain. There were many problems for the American lawyer to deal with in France. The French wanted to limit the territory of the American colonies. England still had 10,000 troops on American soil. Every American war ship was damaged or destroyed. The Continental Army was falling apart—men deserted to return to their homes. Plus, Spain wanted to continue fighting over other issues.

Franklin had been negotiating with France for years. But he was not as careful as he could have been. For years, his personal assistant was spying for the English. And Franklin did not write in the precise language needed for such a serious treaty. So, while Franklin laid down the terms of British surrender, Jay, the tough-minded lawyer, spelled out the terms in exacting detail.

When Franklin became ill with gout and kidney stones, Jay took over. After two years of fighting over land claims and wording, the Treaty of Paris was signed in 1783.

A victorious John Jay returned to New York in July 1784. It had been eight years since he had seen his native city. He was shocked to find the city was in ruins after the war. It was full of gutted and burned buildings. Even more shocking, upon his arrival home, Jay learned he had been appointed by Congress as the new Secretary of Foreign Affairs.

An unfinished painting by Benjamin West of the Treaty of Paris. From left to right: John Jay, John Adams, Benjamin Franklin, Henry Laurens, and William Temple Franklin.

The New Constitution

T HE UNITED STATES OF AMERICA had become a different country since Jay left. Its land size had doubled thanks to the Paris Peace Treaty. By 1790, the population would double to four million. Locks, canals, and bridges spanned rivers. However, there were still old problems that refused to go away.

Congress was shackled by its lack of power. It could not collect taxes. States collected taxes, but would not share them with the federal government. Congress had no control over business. It lacked the funds to pay the army or rebuild the navy. British and Spanish soldiers still held control over American territories in the south and the west. Shooting wars broke out between the states. At one point, Pennsylvania and Virginia fought each other over the Pittsburgh region. In addition to all of that, the United States was $40 million in debt.

The Constitutional Convention of 1787,
at Independence Hall in Philadelphia.

John Jay was convinced that a new constitution
was the only way to save America. A Constitutional
Convention was called in May 1787. The
convention addressed problems facing the United
States. Jay had political enemies who did not want
him to attend the convention. He was never elected
to represent New York when the United States
Constitution was written. To his foes, it didn't
matter that he strongly supported it.

Once the ink was dry on the Constitution, nine of the 13 states had to ratify (approve) it. Then it would become law. To get people to vote for the Constitution, they needed it explained to them. Jay, along with Alexander Hamilton, proposed a series of articles about the Constitution.

The Federalist is the title of the 85 essays that were written. They were signed by the anonymous author "Publius" and published from 1787 to 1788 in various New York newspapers. The purpose of *The Federalist* was to convince New York voters to support ratification of the new Constitution of the United States. Although the authorship of certain essays is still unknown, it is believed that John Jay wrote five essays, Alexander Hamilton 52, and James Madison 28.

Unfortunately, the essays failed in their purpose in New York. The state voted against ratification. However, the papers are still read today by students, scholars, politicians, and anyone who wants to study the meaning of the Constitution.

Facing page: Independence Hall in Philadelphia, site of the Constitutional Convention of 1787.

Setting Up the State Department

NEW YORK EVENTUALLY ratified the Constitution on July 26, 1788. John Jay spent long hours convincing the New York legislature to adopt the document. It went into effect in March 1789. New Yorkers celebrated by ringing church bells and firing cannons at sunrise, noon, and sunset. In April, George Washington was elected as the first president of the United States.

Washington needed help setting up the new Department of State. He called upon John Jay, who had so much experience with foreign affairs. Jay's State Department gave great power to the president to conduct foreign business with little interference from Congress. (A power the president has to this day.) Jay was the temporary secretary of state until Thomas Jefferson took over the job in March 1790.

Facing page: George Washington, first president of the United States.

The Chief Justice

THE CONSTITUTION was an untried, unproven document. It gave power to three branches of government. The legislative branch was the House of Representatives and the Senate. They were to make the laws. The executive branch was the president and his cabinet, such as the secretary of state. They were to make sure the laws were carried out. The third branch was the judiciary. Federal judges and Supreme Court judges made sure the laws passed by Congress were constitutional. That meant that the laws were legal under the wording of the Constitution.

When Washington picked John Jay as the first chief justice to the Supreme Court, he wrote to Jay: "In nominating you I not only acted in my best judgment, but I trust I did a grateful thing to the good citizens of these United States."

The Supreme Court building in Washington, D.C.

As chief justice, Jay was to oversee the six-judge court. The first meeting of the Supreme Court was held in New York City on February 1, 1790. Since the country was brand new, there were no cases to hear that day.

In the early days of the Supreme Court, judges had to travel to various towns to hear cases. This was called the Circuit Court. It was divided into three circuits—Eastern, Middle, and Southern.

Judges had to hold Circuit Court twice a year in each district. The framers of the Constitution did this so that people in every state would see the great dignity of the federal courts. Federal judges were given the power to decide if state laws were constitutional.

The labor of Circuit Court travel quickly upset the Supreme Court judges. They spent months away from their families. They had to travel vast distances by horse, coach, and even on foot. The rooming houses along the way were often dirty rooms filled with bugs, fleas, and poor food. Sickness and bad roads regularly delayed important cases.

Jay found the travel so unpleasant he began looking for another job by 1792. When some friends suggested he run for governor of New York, he accepted. Jay, however, lost the election and stayed as a justice on the Supreme Court.

Chief Justice John Jay of the United States
Supreme Court.

Troubles Across the Ocean

TROUBLES WERE ONCE AGAIN brewing between England and France. Back in 1789, the French people began fighting a revolution based on the American Revolution. The war quickly escalated. There was massive bloodshed in the streets of Paris. The French revolutionaries even chopped off the head of their king.

Some Americans supported the French. Like Jefferson, they believed that the government should be run by common citizens, farmers, and anyone else who could do the job. These people, mostly southerners, called themselves Republicans.

Some, like George Washington and John Jay, felt that government should be run by bankers, lawyers, and businessmen. These men, most of them from northern states, called themselves Federalists. Many Federalists were engaged in trade with England.

When France declared war on England in 1793, the Republicans and the Federalists were deeply divided over the issue. By that time, most Americans were horrified by the bloodiness of the French Revolution. But the United States was still an ally with France. The French expected help in their war against England.

Fighting breaks out in the streets during the French Revolution.

Special Envoy

MEANWHILE, THE BRITISH were taking illegal actions against Americans. In the western territories, the British government had refused to leave the forts on the frontier. And some believed the British were helping Native Americans attack American settlers. In other matters, the British began capturing American ships at sea. They stole the cargo and forced the American sailors to fight in the British navy against France.

France demanded that the United States go to war against Great Britain, but Washington was in no mood for another war. In addition, the United States was once again a strong trading partner with England. Washington knew he could not cut off that trade without harming the American economy. He wanted the United States to remain neutral.

In April 1794, Washington asked Jay to serve as a special envoy to Great Britain. Once again John Jay crossed the ocean—this time to London. On November 19, 1794, Jay signed a treaty with Great Britain that proved profitable to the new

Americans are kidnapped and forced to serve in the British navy against France.

American nation. First, the British agreed to leave the forts on the American frontier. Next, Jay secured America's right to trade in the British West Indies.

By turning aside the threat of war, Jay's Treaty ensured English-American trade. The customs taxes collected through this trade arrangement provided the United States federal government with much-needed funding. Jay's Treaty did nothing, however, to solve the actions taken by the British navy against American sailors.

Burning John Jay

I N THE EARLY DAYS of the United States, there were no long campaigns for political office. While Jay was in London, he was nominated and elected as governor of New York. He was told of this as he was getting off the boat on his return to New York.

Jay's Treaty was strongly opposed by the Republicans in Congress who supported the French. They wanted a war, not peace, with England. Many newspapers ran violently worded editorials against the treaty and Jay. Average citizens joined in violent objections. Jay was burned in effigy in dozens of cities. Copies of Jay's Treaty were burned in the street. Newspaper articles cursed Jay. British businesses had bricks thrown through their windows. In some places, flags were lowered to half-mast in protest.

John Jay was considered a traitor by some Americans when he signed a treaty with England.

Although opposed by many, Jay's Treaty was eventually approved by Congress. When Washington signed the document, demonstrations started again. More effigies of Jay were burned. On September 11, 1795, riots broke out in Boston. Jay was called "the arch-traitor." Washington was called the man who "had completed the destruction of American freedom."

Jay knew the Republicans would oppose his treaty. He didn't care. Even as people were burning his effigy in the streets, he wrote, "We must take men and things as they are, and enjoy all the good we meet with."

Jay had resigned as chief justice on June 29, 1795. Two days later he was sworn in as New York's governor. His main reason for taking the governor's job was to be near his family once again. He was hoping for a peaceful life, but the protests of Jay's Treaty ended this hope.

Jay's term as governor proved to be highly successful. In 1798, he was ready to retire, but he was elected once again. During his second term, Jay pushed through a bill outlawing slavery in New York State.

In 1800, Jay was once again ready to retire. However, President John Adams, preparing himself to leave office, asked Jay to return as chief justice of the Supreme Court. Jay, remembering his travels on the Circuit Court, refused the appointment.

Facing page: two escaped slaves posed for this portrait around 1862. During his second term as governor, John Jay pushed through a bill outlawing slavery in New York State.

The Final Days

IN 1801, JAY AND HIS WIFE built a home on a large piece of land near Hudson. It was a two-day journey from New York City, and mail came only once a week. Their quiet happiness was shattered when Mrs. Jay died in 1802.

As he grew older, historians and scholars who wanted to learn about the Revolution often visited Jay. In 1826, America celebrated the 50th anniversary of the Declaration of Independence. Eighty-year-old Jay was invited to attend ceremonies, but he was too weak to travel. In an odd twist of fate, Thomas Jefferson and John Adams both died on that Fourth of July in 1826. John Jay became the last surviving member of the First Continental Congress.

John Jay died on May 17, 1829. He was 83 years old. As a last request he wrote: "I would have my funeral decent, but not ostentatious [showy]. Instead thereof, I give two hundred dollars to any one poor deserving widow or orphan of this town, whom my children shall select."

John Jay's home near Hudson, New York.

Conclusion

JOHN JAY WAS ONE OF THE GREAT legal minds of his time. He was a moderate man and a peacemaker. He had the education and genius to negotiate complicated treaties with Great Britain. He applied his talents for his country, not his own personal gain. Above it all, John Jay served the people, sometimes under very harsh conditions. Jay's beliefs may best be summed up by the letter he wrote as thousands of people were burning his effigy in the streets:

"...our country possesses a greater portion of information and morals than almost any other people; and although they may for a time be mislead and deceived, there is reason to expect that truth and justice cannot be long hid from their eyes."

Facing page: a portrait of John Jay.

Timeline

Dec. 12, 1745 ..... John Jay born in New York City, New York.

1760 .... Enters King's College (now Columbia University) in New York City.

1764 .... Takes a job as a law clerk in the offices of lawyer Benjamin Kissam.

1768 .... Receives his license to practice law.

1774 .... Marries Sarah Van Brugh Livingston.

Joins the New York Sons of Liberty group known as the Committee of 51.

Becomes a New York delegate to the First Continental Congress.

1775 .... Delegate to the Second Continental Congress. Writes the Olive Branch Petition to send to England's King George III, asking for peace.

1778 .... Delegate and elected president of Continental Congress.

1779 .... Minister to Spain.

1781 .... Goes to France to assist Benjamin Franklin to make peace with Great Britain.

1783 .... Successfully sees the Treaty of Paris signed.

1784 .... Elected as Secretary of Foreign Affairs by Congress.

1788 .... Writes several essays urging the ratification of the Constitution. They will be collected and published in a book called *The Federalist*.

1789 .... First chief justice of the Supreme Court of the United States.

1794 .... Special envoy to Great Britain. Gets the "Jay Treaty" signed.

1795 .... Elected Governor of New York.

May 17, 1829 ..... John Jay dies at his home in Bedford, New York, at age 83.

Where on the Web?

America's Story from America's Library
http://www.americaslibrary.gov/pages/
jb_1212_johnjay_1.html

Compton's Encyclopedia
http://www.comptons.com/encyclopedia/
ARTICLES/0075/00957696_A.html

Info Please
http://www.infoplease.com/ce6/people/
A0826053.html

Discovery School's A-to-Z History
http://school.discovery.com/homeworkhelp/
worldbook/atozhistory/j/286420.html

Rebels With A Vision
http://www.rebelswithavision.com/johnjay.net/

U.S. History.org
http://www.ushistory.org/declaration/related/
jay.htm

Glossary

American Revolution: the war between Great Britain and its American colonies that lasted from 1775 to 1783. America won its independence in the war.

boycott: to try to change the actions of a company or government by refusing to buy their products.

The colonies: the British territories that made up the first 13 states of the United States. The 13 colonies included New Hampshire, Massachusetts, Rhode Island, Connecticut, New York, New Jersey, Pennsylvania, Delaware, Maryland, Virginia, North Carolina, South Carolina, and Georgia.

Constitution: the document that spells out the principles and laws governing the United States.

Constitutional Convention: the meeting of men who wrote the United States Constitution.

Continental Army: the army that fought the British in the Revolutionary War.

Continental Congress: lawmakers who governed the 13 colonies after they declared their independence from Great Britain.

Declaration of Independence: the document written by Thomas Jefferson that declared America's independence from Great Britain.

effigy: a stuffed dummy meant to symbolize a living person.

Federalist: a political party that favors a strong central government over the states.

House of Representatives: a governing body elected by popular vote to rule a nation.

legislature: a body of persons with the power to make, change, or repeal laws.

militia: a group of citizens enrolled in military service during a time of emergency.

Index